HOORAY FOR FARMERS!

by Kurt Waldendorf

BUMBA BOOKS™

LERNER PUBLICATIONS ◆ MINNEAPOLIS

Note to Educators:

Throughout this book, you'll find critical thinking questions. These can be used to engage young readers in thinking critically about the topic and in using the text and photos to do so.

Lerner Publications Company
A division of Lerner Publishing Group, Inc.
241 First Avenue North
Minneapolis, MN 55401 USA

For reading levels and more information, look up this title at www.lernerbooks.com.

Library of Congress Cataloging-in-Publication Data

Names: Waldendorf, Kurt, author.
Title: Hooray for farmers! / by Kurt Waldendorf.
Other titles: Hooray for community helpers!
Description: Minneapolis : Lerner Publications, [2016] | Series: Bumba books— Hooray for community helpers! | Includes bibliographical references and index.
Identifiers: LCCN 2016001070 (print) | LCCN 2016002239 (ebook) | ISBN 9781512414431 (lb : alk. paper) | ISBN 9781512414776 (pb : alk. paper) | ISBN 9781512414783 (eb pdf)
Subjects: LCSH: Farmers—Juvenile literature.
Classification: LCC S519 .W33 2016 (print) | LCC S519 (ebook) | DDC 630.92—dc23

LC record available at http://lccn.loc.gov/2016001070

Manufactured in the United States of America
1 – VP – 7/15/16

LERNER
SOURCE

Expand learning beyond the printed book. Download free, complementary educational resources for this book from our website, www.lernerresource.com.

Table of
Contents

Farmers

Farmers help plants and animals grow.

They work on farms.

Farms use lots of land.

Farmers plant crops

on this land.

Animals live on the

land too.

Farmers use big machines.

This farmer pulls a plow

with a tractor.

The plow gets the ground ready

for seeds.

Why do you think farmers might need big machines?

Seeds grow into crops.

Corn grows high out of

the ground.

Farmers use a combine

to pick the corn.

Some farmers do not need machines.

This farmer uses her hands.

She collects chicken eggs.

Farmers take care of animals.

The animals grow from babies

to adults.

Farmers keep the animals healthy.

This farmer feeds a baby pig.

What other ways do you think farmers care for their animals?

Farmers provide the food we eat. We eat eggs and meat from chickens. We eat the corn that grows in fields.

What other foods do farmers grow?

Farmers know a lot about farm animals and crops.

They learn from other farmers.

Other people go to college to learn too.

Farming is hard work.

Farmers wake up early

to care for animals.

They work all day long.

Farmer Tools

plow

tractor

combine

seeds

Picture Glossary

collects

gathers or picks things

combine

a machine that collects crops

crops

plants grown for food or goods

plow

a machine that digs up soil

23

Index

Read More

Jeffries, Joyce. *Meet the Farmer.* New York: Gareth Stevens, 2014.

Meister, Cari. *Farmers.* Minneapolis: Bullfrog Books, 2015.

Siemens, Jared. *Farmer.* New York: AV2 by Weigl, 2015.

Photo Credits

The images in this book are used with the permission of: © emholk/iStock.com, p. 5; © MaxyM/ Shutterstock.com, pp. 6–7; © tanger/Shutterstock.com, pp. 9, 23 (bottom right); © Jan van Broekhoven/ Shutterstock.com, pp. 10–11, 23 (top right); © Phovoir/Shutterstock.com, pp. 12, 23 (top left); © andresr/ iStock.com, p. 15; © Monkey Business Images/Shutterstock.com, p. 16; © simonkr/iStock.com, p. 19; © Air Images/Shutterstock.com, pp. 20–21; © Charles Brutlag/Shutterstock.com, p. 22 (top); © stefan11/ Shutterstock.com, p. 22 (bottom right); © Ekaterina Lin/Shutterstock.com, p. 22 (bottom left); © Sea Wave/Shutterstock.com, p. 23 (bottom left).

Front Cover: © Alexander Raths/Shutterstock.com.

Who makes a difference in your community? All kinds of helpers are part of your community.

BUMBA BOOKS

BUMBA BOOKS™ HOORAY FOR COMMUNITY HELPERS!

HOORAY FOR
CHEFS!

HOORAY FOR
PILOTS!

HOORAY FOR
CONSTRUCTION
WORKERS!

HOORAY FOR
POLICE
OFFICERS!

HOORAY FOR
FARMERS!

HOORAY FOR
TEACHERS!

HOORAY FOR
NURSES!

HOORAY FOR
VETERINARIANS!

LernerClassroom™
A division of Lerner Publishing Group
www.lernerbooks.com
004–008 Guided Reading: J
Early Intervention: 18*
*Estimated

ISBN 978-1-5124-1477-6

90000

9 781512 414776

Tundra habitats are found in far northern Europe.

Europe also has tundras, plains, mountains, and dry scrubland habitats. In the mountains, there are brown bears and chamois. Polar bears and arctic foxes live in the tundra of northern Europe. Deer and golden jackals can live in nearly any habitat.

Europe's Endangered Animals

Europeans have been working to **protect** habitats and to save animals that are in danger of dying out. The animals on these pages are some of the animals that still need help.

MAP KEY

- European Mink
- Giant Sturgeon
- Angel Shark
- Iberian Lynx
- Mediterranean Monk Seal

European Mink

1. Angel Shark

Angel sharks are flat sharks. These sharks were once widespread in the waters around Europe. Today they are almost gone.

2. Giant Sturgeon

Giant sturgeons can live to be more than 100 years old. These large fish have become extinct in many of the places they once lived. Today they are critically endangered in their remaining habitats.

3. Iberian Lynx

The Iberian lynx is the most endangered cat species on Earth. If the numbers keep dropping, the Iberian lynx could be the first cat species to become extinct in 2,000 years.

Europe

1. SLOVAKIA
2. SLOVENIA
3. ALBANIA
4. MACEDONIA
5. GREECE
6. KOSOVO
7. MONTENEGRO
8. BOSNIA-HERZEGOVINA
9. SERBIA
10. BULGARIA
11. MOLDOVA
12. LUXEMBOURG
13. LIECHTENSTEIN
14. SWITZERLAND
15. AUSTRIA
16. ESTONIA
17. LITHUANIA

4. European Mink

European mink are known for their soft, beautiful fur. Today there are thought to be between 100 and 1,000 of these animals left in the wild.

5. Mediterranean Monk Seal

These dark-colored seals were once found throughout the Mediterranean Sea. Today, there are fewer than 500 Mediterranean monk seals left.

Angel Shark

The angel shark lives on the seafloor in the waters off of Europe and North Africa. During the day it hides itself in the sand with just its eyes poking out. At night it hunts for bony fish, skates, squid, and shellfish.

Angel sharks are often killed when they get tangled up in fishing nets meant to catch other

Angel sharks eat all kinds of shellfish, such as the lobster shown here.

Angel sharks spend most of their time swimming along the seafloor.

Fishermen often use nets to gather fish. Sometimes angel sharks get tangled in these nets and die.

fish. It is hard for scientists to know the real number of angel sharks left. However, they guess that it is fewer than 1,400 fish. These sharks are listed as critically endangered. People in Europe are doing what they can to save this species.

Giant Sturgeon

Giant sturgeons live in the Caspian Sea and the Black Sea. The eggs of these fish are thought of as a special treat. People like them so much that many fishermen caught these fish. Giant sturgeons are now in danger of becoming extinct in the wild because so many were caught. Though giant sturgeons are protected, they are still caught in nets by mistake. They are also **poached**.

The giant sturgeon's eggs are known as caviar. Caviar is thought of as a special treat by many people.

Giant sturgeons have another problem besides fishing. These fish return to the rivers where they were born to **breed**. When these rivers are dammed, the fish cannot get to their **spawning** grounds.

European Mink

Mink are known for their beautiful fur. European mink live mostly in eastern Europe. They live on river and stream banks where they dig burrows in which to sleep. They come out at night to hunt. They eat small animals, frogs, shellfish, fish, and bugs.

One of the biggest dangers for mink is habitat loss. Rivers and streams are being dammed and polluted. Another problem for the European mink is the American mink, which is not a native species. The American mink was introduced in Europe and now competes with the smaller European mink for food and habitat.

Mink have poor eyesight, so they use their strong sense of smell to find prey when they are hunting.

Iberian Lynx

The Iberian lynx is a spotted wildcat. It has a short tail, ear tufts, and longer fur on the sides of its face. Iberian lynx live in the southern parts of Portugal and Spain. They like forests or land with plenty of bushes for hiding. They eat mostly rabbits.

These animals are critically endangered. It is believed that there are only between 84 and 143 Iberian lynx left.

The Iberian lynx is related to the bobcat, the Eurasian lynx, and the Canadian lynx.

The Iberian lynx lives in the hot, dry climates of southern Portugal and Spain. Shown here are mountains in Andalusia, in southern Spain.

Rabbits make up a large part of what the Iberian lynx eats.

They are dying out because of habitat loss. They are also dying because there are fewer rabbits due to hunting and illnesses.

Mediterranean Monk Seal

The Mediterranean monk seal lives around the Mediterranean Sea. These monk seals also live in small groups in waters off of Morocco, in the Ionian and Aegean seas, and off the coasts of Greece and Turkey. There are only about 350 to 450 Mediterranean monk seals left in the world.

Mediterranean monk seals give birth in sea caves like the one shown here.

Mediterranean monk seals eat fish and shellfish, including octopuses, squid, and eels.

Monk seals used to gather and have babies on open beaches around the Mediterranean. Today, however, they give birth in sea caves. Mediterranean monk seal numbers have gone down due to fishing and sealing. A large number of seals also died because of **toxic algal blooms** in the seawater.

Save Europe's Endangered Animals!

Europe is a small continent with lots of people. All these people need space to live, roads to drive on, and land for farming. This means people are often in **conflict** with the wildlife in Europe. People take over the natural habitat plants and animals need to live.

Most Europeans now know that it is important to keep Europe's **biodiversity** safe. People have been working for many years to educate people, protect Europe's wild places, and help animals that are in trouble. There is still a lot of work to do, but there is hope for Europe's endangered animals!

ADAPT (uh-DAPT) To change to fit requirements.

BIODIVERSITY (by-oh-dih-VER-sih-tee) The number of different types of living things that are found in a certain place on Earth.

BREED (BREED) To make babies.

CONFLICT (KON-flikt) A fight or a struggle.

DECIDUOUS (deh-SIH-joo-us) Having leaves that fall off every year.

HABITATS (HA-beh-tats) The kinds of land where animals or plants naturally live.

POACHED (POHCHD) Hunted animals when it was against the law.

POPULATION (pop-yoo-LAY-shun) A group of animals or people living in the same area.

PROTECT (pruh-TEKT) To keep safe.

SPAWNING (SPAWN-ing) Coming together to lay eggs.

TEMPERATE (TEM-puh-rut) Not too hot or too cold.

TOXIC ALGAL BLOOMS (TOK-sik AL-gul BLOOMZ) Events in which many plantlike living things without roots or stems that live in water produce poisons or matter that can hurt other living things.

Index

C
continent(s), 4, 6, 22

E
Europeans, 10, 22

F
fish, 10, 12–16
forests, 5, 8, 18

H
habitat(s), 5, 8–10, 17, 22

I
Italy, 7

L
land, 4, 8, 18, 22

M
mountains, 5, 9

P
plants, 5, 22
population, 4
Portugal, 7, 18

R
river(s), 15–17
roads, 5, 22

S
Spain, 7, 18

T
toxic algal blooms, 21

W
water(s), 6, 10, 12, 20

Web Sites

Due to the changing nature of Internet links, PowerKids Press has developed an online list of Web sites related to the subject of this book. This site is updated regularly. Please use this link to access the list: www.powerkidslinks.com/sea/europe/